# Witchery

By
Lily Oak

I0190781

# Witchery

ISBN 978-1-9079-6300-1

Published by

## Hedge Witchery Books

www.hedge-witcherybooks.com

Copyright © Lindsay Caulfield 2010

All rights reserved. No part of this publication may be reproduced, stored in a retrieval system, or transmitted in any form or by any means, electronic, mechanical, photocopying, recording or otherwise, without the prior permission of the copyright owner.

# Index

# Hello,

Just a quick note on how this little book came into being. A year or two ago I found myself being asked over and over for basic information on witchcraft. Usually from people who were just becoming interested in it, and wanted a simple outline before they really got stuck into the mountain of information available. Initially, after re-sending the same information a dozen times, I typed up the notes I'd taken when I first began to learn about witchcraft and put together a couple of very short guides. Since then the information has been re-written and produced as a series of online articles. Now, after a few nudges from various people they are returning in print. This tiny little book is a very basic guide to getting started with witchcraft and spell casting, and hopefully will provide a starting point from which to expand from.

*Lily*

# What is Magic?

If you are reading this expecting long mysterious explanations of cryptic ceremonies used to conjure magic, I am afraid I am about to disappoint you.

What is magic? Everything.

Where is magic? Everywhere.

You just have to learn to see it. For me at least, magic isn't something we create it is something we use. A type of energy given of by every natural thing. Think more Lyra's dust, than Mr Potters Wand. Just as all natural things differ in species, mineral type, personality, etc, so does the magic they radiate. From the purification properties of copal, to the deep passions inspired by garnet.

Sometimes these magic energies combine in a way that jumps out at us, makes itself so tangible that even the most stoic of sceptics would struggle to deny it. The moment the dipping sun hits the right spot on the horizon to flood the sky crimson. Sunlight catching dew drops on unfurling ferns in spring. Frost encased spiders webs on crisp autumn morns.

It is how magic is utilised that gives us the diverse make-up of witchcraft and spell casting that we have today. Every path and every individual practitioner has a different way of connecting to these energies, that is as unique as each of us are as individuals. The different magical energies can also be related to in different ways by different people, a lot of people find that despite every book on spell casting they have ever read saying a particular crystal carries one type of magic, they pick up another from it. Of course there will be large similarities between some, otherwise group work and covens would not work as well as they do. And then there are others that prefer keeping their workings private and something they only share with themselves.

Due to witchcraft being a lot more publicly discussed than it once was, practitioners are now able to talk about the way they see magic, discuss their path, it's history and it's beliefs. This enables us to not only look at what magic is to ourselves, but also what it s to others. It allows our perspective of what magic is to be challenged and learn and grow because of it.

Magic is something that affects all of us whether we choose to work with it or not, at some point in your life, no matter what your views on witchcraft or spell casting, you'll be affected by magic.

# Altars

Altars have many uses within witchcraft, they can be used in spells, as a way to display the turning of the Wheel of the Year, or just as a place for contemplation and meditation.

Altars can vary in size and form as much as magic practitioners themselves do. They can be a small wooden box containing a few items, right up to a 6 by 4 foot carved oak slab. I've seen many altars set up on windowsills, shelves, bedside tables and mantelpieces. Altars also do not need to be in a fixed place, or permanent. Tree stumps make excellent outdoor altars (just be careful with any candles).

The important thing is to stop worrying about how your altar *should* look, and think about what you actually want an altar for. There are a few things that a lot of altars do include, but an altar is your personal work space, and it should include what you feel necessary, not what anybody else does.

~

Below are a few things that you typically find on an altar;

Elemental representations - These can be anything that represent Earth, Air, Fire and Water. These do not have to be anything elaborate it could be, a small crystal or bowl of soil for Earth, a feather or incense for Air, a candle for Fire and a small cup of rain/stream water or a sea shell for Water.

Deity representations - Statues or pictures of a specific Deity. If you are not working with a specific God or Goddess then you may still want to light candles or have representations of general male and female energies.

Seasonal representations - Foliage, flowers and symbols representing the time of year, especially if your altar is set-up to celebrate one of the Wheel of the Year festivals.

Pentacle or Pentagram - Often people put a Pentacle or Pentagram at the centre of their altar. This is often either as a tile or sewn onto an altar cloth. On smaller altars you could paint one on a pebble or shell.

Magical tools and diaries - If people have tools they use for magical purposes, wands, runes, athame, tarot decks, crystals, etc, then they often like to leave these displayed on permanent altars. Even if you do not have a permanent altar leaving these tools on your altar (especially during a full moon) can be a simple way of cleansing them.

This is by no means any kind of definitive list, you can put anything on your altar that you feel has a significant meaning to you. Have fun with it remember that setting up and maintaining your altar should be something that you enjoy, not something to worry about or view as a chore.

# Circle Casting

Casting circles for spells and rituals is something practiced by many branches of witchcraft and Paganism. The purpose and necessity of casting a circle is something that will vary between practitioners and paths.

Some believe that circles are cast to create a protected area in which to practice magic. Others see them as a way of building magical power and focusing it into the ritual that is being carried out. There are others that believe they are a way of acknowledging, paying respect to, and thanking the deities and magical energies that are present during rituals and spells.

As you can imagine, due to the difference in beliefs as to what a circle is for, there is also a large sliding scale as to how important and elaborate a part of rituals it becomes.

Personally, as a Hedge Witch, circle casting as we know it today isn't really a big part of my chosen path, but it's still something I often do. Granted I do so in a very short simple format, but I find it creates a nice start and finish point to spells. This may sound a little strange but after a day at the office or running round after children having something you do as a regular prelude to workings is a good way to enter the right mind-set and clear away the cluttered thoughts that may disrupt your concentration.

Below is a very simple example of circle casting, as with all magical workings it's best to come up with your own adaptation and make it personal to you.

The circle itself may or may not be marked out physically. This can be done with anything you choose but rope and salt are common choices. Sometimes candles are used to mark the directional correspondences on the circumference of the circle, (Green for North, Yellow for East, Red for South and Blue for West). Sometimes representations of each element are used to mark directional correspondences, either around the circumference or on an altar within the circle, (Earth for North, Air for East, Fire for South and Water for West).

Before the circle is cast the person leading the ritual will welcome the Lord and Lady, or specific deities that they wish to be present.

They will then walk round the edge of the circle in a clockwise direction (traditionally starting at the East) marking it out with either an athame, a staff, a wand or simply their finger. They may stop at each compass point to welcome the energies / God / watchtower, or they may complete the circle and then welcome them. An example of what they may say would be:

"Energies of the East, I ask you watch over this rite with powers of knowledge and communication, guided by Air, I bid you 'Hail and Welcome',
Energies of the South, I ask you to watch over this rite with powers of strength and will, guided by Fire, I bid you 'Hail and Welcome',
Energies of the West, I ask you to watch over this rite with powers of peace and emotion, guided by Water, I bid you 'Hail and Welcome',
Energies of the North, I ask you to watch over this rite with powers of prosperity and stability, guided by Earth, I bid you 'Hail and Welcome'."

Once the circle is cast it is generally believed you should not cross it's boundary, and break the circle, if it can at all be helped. Some practitioners will cut a doorway in the circle if someone needs to leave, by using whatever they used to draw the circle to mark two small lines across the boundary of it. Once the person has left / re-entered they then re-connect the two edges.

One, if not the, most important part of casting a circle is for all the participants to visualise it as clearly as they can. For most people this will be a circular wall or sphere of light, but it is a very personal thing and will vary for everyone.

Once the spell or ritual has been complete, it is important to then take down the circle. Confusingly this is often called 'opening' the circle as people often visualise the energy or light dissipating outwards, rather than falling in on itself.

To do this the person leading the ritual will walk around the circumference in an anticlockwise direction tracing the outline of the circle. Either whilst they are walking and reach the compass points, or after they have finished they will say something along the lines of:

"Energies of the East, thank you for joining me in this rite, stay if you can, go if you must, I bid you 'Hail and Farewell',
Energies of the North, thank you for joining me in this rite, stay if you can go if you must, I bid you 'Hail and Farewell',
Energies of the West, thank you for joining me in this rite, stay if you can go if you must, I bid you 'Hail and Farewell'
Energies of the South, thank you for joining me in this rite, stay if you can go if you must, I bid you 'Hail and Farewell'."

They will often use a similar statement format for thanking and saying goodbye to the Lord and Lady or other deities, which they will do next.

As I said previously this is a basic outline of how circles are cast. Some are much more complicated, and by the same token some are much simpler. Some plainly consist of  visualising the circle and mentally acknowledging the different elements and directions associated with them.

However you choose to embrace this practice, like all things magical, it will develop personal power and meaning the more you do it.

# Candle Magic

Candles are a staple tool of any magical practitioner and candle magic is a wonderfully simple way to cast spells. When I first started practicing witchcraft it was the first type of spell I learnt. It is also very easy to personalise, and after all if we can't personally connect with the spell we are casting then it is unlikely to be successful. The use of candles can also be incorporated into larger rituals, in fact I can't remember being at any ritual that didn't include candles in some way shape or form.

Firstly you need to select a candle in an appropriate colour, colour correspondences will differ for everyone you may get a different set of energies from one colour than most people do, use what feels right for you. Below is a list of the more commonly used correspondences;

White - Healing, peace, clarity, clearing.

Black - Banishing, ending negativity, stopping destructive forces.

Pink - Empowerment, happiness, joy, healing loved ones, ending conflicts.

Red - Empowerment, passion, strength, courage, control, protection.

Purple - Psychic visions.

Dark Blue - Psychic awareness and dreams.

Light Blue - Healing, protection.

Yellow - Energizing, mental stimulation.

Orange - Energizing, physical stimulation.

Green - Prosperity, abundance, career, money, fertility.

Once you have your candle you need charge it with what you wish to happen, again there are many different ways to do this but often the easiest one to start with is by writing on the candle what you would like the outcome of the spell to be.

Another thing that is often effective in candle magic is dressing the candle with oil. There are hundreds of essential oils out there, each with a different set of magical make-up. Either pick one specific to the type of spell you are casting or go for something like Frankincense, which is often used generally for meditations, and will assist in your visualization of your desired outcome.

Then, sit quietly and visualize what you have asked for happening as clearly as you can. Lots of people struggle to visualize clearly without their mind wondering. Try to use your own individual strengths for spell casting. If you like art, draw a representation of your desired outcome If you write poetry write a poem about your desired outcome, etc.

Now light the candle, as you watch it burn visualize what you have written rising with the flame and floating of into the world and trust that what you have asked for will be granted to you.

# Crystals

Crystals are a valuable and very versatile tool. You can wear them as a talisman, place them on alters and incorporate them in to spells. Below is a list of my favourites and how I use them. As with all magical correspondences the below list is by no means set in stone, there is every possibility that a particular crystal will present you with an entirely different set of energies to the associated ones I've described. Work with what feels right for you, our connection with magical energies is as unique as we are as people so there will always be exceptions to every rule.

Amethyst
Transforming negativity, visions of other plains and soothing.

Amazonite
Truth, communication, trust, creativity, intellect, psychic ability, healing emotional trauma.

Amber
Clarity, joy, calm and confidence.

Aquamarine
Heightens spiritual awareness and allows you to connect to your higher self.

Blue Lace Agate
Spirituality, movement, grace, eases loneliness & loss, healing bone and joint conditions.

Carnelian
Prevents feelings of anger, fear and jealousy. Encourages courage, individuality and helps heal bone and skin conditions and tissue damage.

Citrine
Energizes, rids negativity. Encourages wealth and prosperity.

Clear Quartz
Focuses energy, alters consciousness and links dimensions.

Garnet
Passion, ambition, romantic love, sex, sensuality, persistence, stamina, survival, power, confidence and assertion.

Green Adventurine
Prosperity and financial good luck.

Hematite
Reaching your full potential, enhance mental capabilities, self-control and peace.

Howlite
Relieving pain, stress and rage. Helps reasoning and observation.

Jade
Sends negative energy back to sender, wealth, love and healing.

Kyanite
Psychic ability, visions, clairvoyance, telepathy, lucid dreaming and astral travel.

Labradorite
Intuition, especially in times of conflict or change, protects magic, balancing.

Moonstone
Contacting spirit guides, creativity, calming, intuition, psychic perception, cleansing, repels negative energy and balancing.

Opal
Eases change, encourages imagination and creativity, happy dreams.

Peridot
Marriage, love, luck, peace. Deflects negativity back to sender.

Pyrite
Intellect, memory, wellbeing, guards against negative energy.

Rose Quartz
Healing emotional wounds, love and balancing.

Smokey Quartz
Eliminate and protect from negative energy.

Snowflake Obsidian
Banish grief and aid decision making.

Tigerseye
Female issues, emotional tension and optimism.

Once you have selected the type crystal you are going to work with it is a good idea to cleanse it of any negative/residual energies that have become attached to it either because it's a new tool or due to previous uses or rituals. There are lots of different ways to do this. You can either use one of these methods, or any combination or variation that feels right for the spell you are casting or ritual you are performing.

Use rain, spring or sea water to pour over the crystal or stand the crystal in.

Bury the crystal in earth, sand or salt.

Pass the crystal through incense smoke.

Pass the crystal through/over a flame.

Stand the crystal in moonlight.

Use a citrine crystal to cleanse the crystal you are using, (citrine is unique in that it is believed not to hold on to negative energies).

The more you work with a specific crystal, the more you will feel a personal connection to it and the more effective a tool it becomes.

# Herbs, Plants & Resins

Plants form a integral part of magic. They can be used to decorate places and alters, they can be turned into incense or burnt as smudge sticks.

In an ideal world we would all grow and harvest our own herbs, or forage for wild ones ourselves. If you do decide to go down the route of growing your own I would recommend seeking out one of the specialist books on planting and harvesting by the moon, in order to gain maximum magical energy from them. If you decide to collect plants and herbs from the wild please be respectful of where you collect them from and give something back, collect seed pods from wild plants in that area and scatter them to help the area grow.

It is unlikely that you will be able to grow or collect everything you wish to use yourself, in these cases please use a reputable online retailer that stocks from organic, sustainable sources.

Listed below are my favourites and what I used them for. The magical correspondences given are a good reflection of the generally accepted ones, however as with everything in magic, there will be variations for everyone. As always the more you practice the more you will get a feel for what works best for you.

Birch - Starting anew, clearing away unwanted past influences and offering protection to new ventures.

Borage - Courage, power and strength, particularly psychic strength.

Buttercup - Wealth and abundance, making a risk pay off.

Calendula - Associated with death rites and psychic development.

Cardamom - Love, lust, passion and sex.

Copal - Purification and cleansing.

Coriander - Lust and love. (Seeds can be added to red wine for simple lust potion.)

Dogwood - Silence and protecting secrets.

Dragons Blood - Power, energy, strength and determination. Love and sex. Protection and cleansing. Can be added to any other ingredients to add potency to spells.

Eyebright - Insight, thinking clearly and psychic work.

Fennel - Protection and purification.

Fir Needles - Change, new beginnings, progress, birth and re-birth

Frankincense - Meditation, visions and spiritual growth. Blessing, protection and purification. Love, courage and healing.

Gardenia - Harmony, peace and love.

Ginger - Courage, sex, love and money.

Hawthorn - Fertility, sex and new beginnings. Use in spells for personal growth and in love spells for finding your soul mate.

Hazel - Can grant wishes. Encourages knowledge and wisdom.

Heather - Good luck and spiritual development.

Hops - Sleep, healing and exorcism.

Holly - Protection and strength.

Honeysuckle - Moving on in life, intuitiveness. Increases sexuality.

Ivy - Marriage and fidelity. Protection.

Jasmine - Sex, love and romance. Prophetic visions and dreams. Also used to represent or invoke the moon.

Jericho Flowers - Re-birth, re-kindling love or friendship.

Lavender - Used by women to attract love. Peace, joy and healing.

Mastic - Increase transcendental abilities, psychic ability and clairvoyance.

Meadowsweet - Spells for female issues or involving a bride.

Mugwort - Psychic dreams and visions, Astral projection, lucid dreaming. Protection, strength and healing.

Myrtle - Concentration.

Nettles - Protection, purification and exorcism. Can help in turning a negative situation into a positive one. Recovery after emotional ordeal.

Nutmeg - Energy and good luck. Protection and breaks hexes.

Oak - Healing, protection and strength. Knowledge, intuition and channelling energies. Increases male sexuality and fertility. Helps to increase your social circle.

Osha Root - Wards off and dispels evil.

Palo Santo - Avoiding misfortune, calming and ridding of negative energies.

Parsley - Visions, spells affecting animals and pregnancy related spells.

Peony - Repelling negative energies.

Peppermint - Psychic ability and visionary dreams.

Primrose - Peacefulness, calm and increases creativity and beauty.

Rose - Increase compassion, empathy, beauty and love. Reduces selfish behaviour, promotes a positive domestic atmosphere, brings joy and happiness.

Rowan Berries - Increase magical power.

Rue - Use for protection whilst entering psychic visions, astral projection or contacting spirits. Also used to protect a home from illness.

Saffron - Lifts your spirits and creates a positive attitude.

Sage - Wisdom, longevity, healing and protection.

Salt - Used in consecrations and blessings. Powerful tool for protection and exorcism.

Sandalwood - Sex, meditation and spirituality.

Solomon's seal - Very affective addition to love potions.

Spruce needles - Cleansing, fresh beginnings.

St Johns Wart - Protection, courage and success in disputes.

Storax - Clears negative atmospheres and thoughts, promotes peaceful sleep.

Sulphur - Breaks or prevents curses and hexes, diminishes a enemy's power over you.

Vervain - Insight and visions.

Willow - Use in any spell involving emotions. Helps direct magic and block out stray or background energies. Psychic work.

Wormwood - Reduces anger and other negative emotional responses.

Yew - Re- generation and recovery. Contacting lost friends and family.

Please bear in mind if you do decide to create potions that not all herbs are edible.

For further reading on this I would recommend 'Encyclopaedia of Magical Herbs' by Scott Cunningham.

# The Wheel of the Year

The Wheel of the Year is often used to describe the constantly revolving cycle of the seasons, upon which the Pagan festivals are based on. Dependant on your chosen path within witchcraft or paganism the way you celebrate these events will vary. There are 8 festivals that form the pagan year.

~

Four of them fall on solar solstices or equinoxes, (these are known as the 'lesser sabbats'). These are;

Eostara (around the 21$^{st}$ March)
The Vernal Equinox. This is the day when the light catches up with the darkness, and will grow stronger. It marks a time when male and female energies begin to entwine, it is a time when growth begins. This is the time to think about turning plans into actions. Look at what parts of your life you wish to grow with the coming season, and decide how to best nurture them.

Litha (around the 21$^{st}$ June)
The Summer Solstice, the longest day of the year. As this is the time when the light is strongest, it is seen as a good time to bring forward all those plans you would like to come into fruition. It is known as the night when all wishes are granted. It is often regarded as a time to gather with friends, celebrate life and look towards a generous harvest, not only of the land, but of everything in life we have worked towards.

Mabon (around 21$^{st}$ September)
The Autumn Equinox, the darkness now matches the light again. This is the second of the harvest festivals, and a good time to take stock of the year so far. This can be used as an opportunity to deal with any negative feelings that we wish to release ourselves from before Samhain.

Yule (around 21$^{st}$ December)

The Winter Solstice, the longest night of the year. After the longest night, the hours of daylight slowly begin to increase, Yule celebrations traditionally go on until dawn, to watch the sunrise and celebrate the returning of the light. Pagans often treat this as an opportunity to remember that even in the depths of Winter, eventually the Spring will return.

~

The other four festivals fall between these and are considered days of high spiritually, when the veil is at its thinnest and often used as a way to look forward to the coming season (these are known as the 'greater sabbats'). These are;

Imbolic (2nd February)
The world prepares itself for the coming Spring. Now is the time to look forward, think about what you would like to achieve with the coming year, and make plans as to how you can set this in motion. It is a time to take stock, the moment of contemplation before action. If you are looking to make a change, large or small, now it the time to change the course of your path.

Beltane (30th April - 1st May)
The word Beltane originates from Celtic and Gaelic words meaning 'bright fire', and is celebrated by the lighting of bonfires. It is a celebration of life, the earth is in full bloom and the days are long. It is a time to celebrate all the you have been given and all you have achieved. It is also a time to look at the parts of your life in which you feel less fulfilled and make positive plans to address this. Beltane is also a festival of fertility, when the God and Goddess join together.

Lammas (1st August)
The first of the harvest celebrations and known as the Feast of Bread as the corn harvest begins. It marks a time when crops began to be brought in and preserved for the coming winter months. This can be used as a time to look into what we need to get through the darker times in our lives and be thankful for the resources we have.

# Samhain (31st October)

Sometimes known as pagan new year, the Sun God makes his final sacrifice and the cycle of life and death completes another turn. The veil between worlds is at it's thinnest. A lot of people view this as a time to remember loved one that have passed and acknowledge death as a part of life rather then the end of it. It is also a time to look within, just as plants retreat to the earth for the dark season, we should go inside ourselves and accept what we find, whether it be light or dark, and learn from it. Once we have this knowledge we can then look forward and plan for the future.

~

The exact date of these festivals can vary from year to year, and differ depending on which hemisphere you are in.

~

The Wheel of the Year is also a story of the Earth Goddess and Sun God, (I have chosen to use these particular names for the male and female deities as they are widely used, however they have many other names and forms). I have written a basic version of this age old tale below, but there are many versions to be found and explored.

As Samhain comes around, the Sun God makes his final sacrifice. He sacrifices himself in order that the earth may have the last of his strength and be able to come back to life with the return of the Spring. The Goddess mourns him, but has the continued hope of the light she carries within her womb. At Yule she gives birth and the Sun God is reborn, from this point on the light starts to slowly return to the world. The Goddess returns to the earth to seek rest.

As Imbolic arrives the Sun God is growing stronger and with him the strength of the day, the Goddess returns to the world no longer the Crone, but fully rejuvenated. Eostara marks the day once again overtaking the night, the Sun God reaches maturity and starts to become attracted to the Goddess in her Maiden form. As the Beltane fires burn bright the God and Goddess come together and she begins to carry his light within her.

22

Lammas sees the Sun God at his strongest, but from here on he will give of himself to ensure a bountiful harvest. As we reach Mabon the Sun God is much weakened and the light gives way to the increasing darkness. The Goddess is sad as she knows he will soon be gone from her. And here we reach Samhain again. The wheel has completed one full turn but continues on it's ever ending cycle.

# The Moon

The Moon and it's phases form an integral part of not just spell casting, but a witches life in general. Most witches that have been practicing for any length of time have a rough idea of what the moon phase is without checking a calendar, it's just an instinct you develop over time. It is widely believed that the cycle of the moon has an affect on magical energies. Choosing to wait for the right time to cast a spell can be a great benefit.

~

Waxing to the Full Moon
A waxing moon refers to the time when the moon is growing leading up to the Full Moon. Whilst the moon is increasing you should cast spells that are focused on things and situations which require growth. Once the moon is full this is a good time for casting spells of abundance, fertility and luck.

~

Waning to the New Moon
A waning moon refers to the time when the moon is decreasing in size leading to the New Moon. Whilst the moon is decreasing in size you should cast spells for making things go away, diminishing things and distancing yourself from situations. Once you reach the New Moon you should cast spells for banishing things, new beginnings and starting new projects.

~

There are also monthly significances to the moon. The various names for different moons can vary a lot, but I have listed some of the more commonly used ones below. Some of these are a lot more historical than others, for example 'Blue Moon' and 'Black Moon' only exist because we use the Gregorian calendar.

## Blue Moon
A Blue Moon is the name given to a second full moon occurring in any one calendar month.

## Black Moon
A Black Moon is the name given to a second new moon in any one calendar month.

## Harvest Moon
There are so many different views as to when this is. I have seen it used as a name for the full moon occurring in September, October and November. A widely held opinion it that it is which ever full moon falls closest to Mabon.

## Quiet Moon (January)
All is quiet in the world. The light has began to return but darkness still prevails. The Earth seems to be holding her breath, waiting for the day to become strong enough to begin to beckon life.

## Moon of Ice (February)
This can be viewed as a simple reference to the weather at this time of year. Alternatively, things can often seem bleakest just before the dawn, the world has been still for a long time and is restlessly awaiting Spring, for this reason this moon is also known as Storm Moon.

## Moon of Winds (March)
Again this could be a simple expression of the climate at this time of year. Another view is that it is named this due to wind being representative of change. Look around, bulbs are pushing green spears through the winter trodden earth, the world is in a stage of transition.

## Growing Moon (April)
The sowing season is here. Plant crops under the full Growing Moon for a bumper harvest come Autumn.

## Bright Moon (May)
This is thought to be named due to the bright burning fires of Beltane.

## Moon of Horses (June)

There are a number of different theories as to why June's moon is called this, but the most widely believed seems to be that historically this was the most common time of year for horse fairs and trading.

Claiming Moon (July)

There isn't a lot of information readily available on where this name originated. The few references I did find suggest it was due to a few moons following the romance of Beltane suitors would begin to announce their intentions towards young maidens.

Dispute Moon (August)

This is another moon name which there isn't a huge amount of information written on. The only references I've ever found on it, make reference to July's Claiming Moon, a young girl and her family would often face dilemmas over whether or not she should marry and arguments would start. There is also a school of thought that suggest the name is because the world seems to be at odds with itself the days are shortening towards the Autumn equinox and grain are ripe in the fields but the Sun is still bright in the sky and the weather is warm.

Singing Moon (September)

Named after the singing celebrations of those returning from the fields after much harvesting. It represents a time leading up to Mabon when the toil is almost over and we can rest and enjoy the rewards of our hard work.

Blood Moon (October)

Blood Moon has a large significance for wildlife. It is often the brightest moon of the year and many animals wait for it as a signal to start migration, hence the reason it is also known as Hunters Moon as due to the effect on wildlife it is indeed a very good night to go hunting.

Dark Moon (November)

The equinox has past and the light is getting weaker. The hours the world spends in darkness lengthen as the nights continue to eat into the days.

Cold Moon (December)

The reason for this name is fairly self explanatory. The world is dark as the sun is at it's weakest.

# Creating Spells

There are lots of books written containing spells, and a countless amount of websites devoted to them. My advice regarding spells written by other people has always been, read as many as you can, and take from them the parts that appeal to you. Add things, remove things, switch the crystals or the herbs used, just make it your own. In my opinion spells *always* work best when they are written for a specific person and purpose.

One very important question you should ask yourself before performing any kind of spell is whether or not you should cast it at all. Many braches of magic believe that if you put something negative out there, sooner or later it'll come back to you. This is well illustrated by part of the Wiccan Rede;

"An Ye Harm None, Do What Ye Will"

Usually what I say is ask yourself two questions;
Will this spell directly affect or influence anyone else?
If 'yes', would *I* mind somebody else casting the same spell and affecting *me* in this way?

If your happy that the only way you would directly influence someone is in a way which you can live with, then go ahead with spell. There is much debate around the ethics of spell casting, for example, if you cast a protection spell on your home, and then a burglar breaks there leg whilst trying to break in, does that mean you've 'harmed' them? I always say ethics is a personal thing, and as long as you consider your actions first and are happy with what your doing, then do it.

The next thing you have to decide on is exactly what you want your spell to achieve. Are you looking for something specific to happen? A sick friend making speedy recovery, a new job, etc. Or, you may want to do small ritual just to feel closer to your spirituality, or to celebrate specific festival or moon phase. Whatever you are casting a spell for don't go into it with a vague idea, make sure you have your purpose very clear in your mind before you start.

It is important to prepare yourself for spell casting, to relax, but not feel tired, after all you need to focus and place some enthusiasm into your castings. This is sometimes referred to as 'raising power' or 'building energy'. This can be done by, singing, chanting, dancing, playing musical instruments or meditation. Actually, there are countless ways to do this, just remember what your doing it for, as a way to wake-up the senses and focus them on the spell or ritual you are about to perform.

During your workings it is important that you feel comfortable and will not be disturbed. These are things that should be taken into consideration when deciding on where and when you will perform your ritual.

In my opinion one of the most important parts of any spell comes at the very end. However you choose to finish your spell, you need to invest some confidence in it, have a little faith. Whatever you've cast for try not to overly fret about it. You've cast the spell, you've dealt with it / put it in hands of the Lord and Lady / released it to the universe, however you want to think of it. It sounds a redundant thing to say but, if your going to use magic, you need to believe in it.

# Example Spells

With all the spells remember to prepare the altar or area in which you are working as described previously. Also, remember to finish any workings in a suitable way as previously discussed.

~

This is a very simple spell that could be performed for a sick family member you wanted to aid in a speedy recovery.

This could be done at any moon phase depending how you look at it. If a waning or new moon think about banishing the illness. If a waxing or full moon, think about the persons health growing.

Take a pale blue candle - (pale blue due to its correspondence as a healing colour).

Dress the candle with Frankincense oil - (for love, protection and healing qualities)

Light the candle and imagine the illness draining out off the loved one who is ill. Once you have a clear picture in your mind of them illness free, picture them growing in strength, returning to full health, full of energy.

If you are unable to burn the candle down completely at this time, move it to somewhere where it won't be unattended, where you can continue to light it another day. Maybe, light it for an hour each day, and whenever you look at it, let it remind you of those images of your loved one returned to health.

~

This is a very simple rhyme that can be said aloud or written on a white candle on a full moon, to try and ensure a strife free time ahead;

"Full Moon in the night,
Bathing me in glorious light,
As through the month your light disappears,
Please take with it all of my cares."

~

This spell can be used to banish cares or troublesome situations from your life;

Wait until a waning or new moon.

Light a black candle - (due to black having connections with new starts and ridding of negativity).

Take a piece of paper and pen and write down the details of what is troubling you. As you are writing clearly envisage them in your head, then imagine the images running down your arm and into the ink you are describing them with.

Have a fire-proof bowl ready (this may be a spell best performed outdoors, always be careful when doing spells involving fire).

Light the piece of paper you have written on from the flame of the black candle, and drop it into fire-proof bowl to reduce to ashes. As it burns imagine the thing you are trying to rid yourself from disappearing into ash with it.

If you are unable to burn the black candle down completely at this time, move it to somewhere where it won't be unattended, where you can continue to light it another day. Maybe, light it for an hour each evening, and whenever you look at it imagine your troubles shrieking as the remaining candle does.

~

Now I know what your thinking, that these are all painfully simple. Well as I said at the beginning of this book, magic can be very simple. Use very basic spells as a starting point, and as you get more practiced add to them. Incorporate crystals and add more herbs, use a few different colour candles to really tailor spell to what you need. The thing to remember is that by far and away the most valuable ingredient to any spell or ritual is your own thought, creativity and will. There are countless books and online resources available for you to build your knowledge from, but only make a spell as long and detailed as you feel you will be able to hold focus for. As I've said many times throughout this little book, do what feels right for you.

Happy Castings.

www.ingramcontent.com/pod-product-compliance
Lightning Source LLC
Chambersburg PA
CBHW071803020426
42331CB00008B/2385